MASTER THE MEDIA

THE STEP-BY-STEP GUIDE TO ELEVATING YOUR BRAND ON AIR, ON CAMERA AND ON STAGE

ZAKIYA LARRY

TO: _____

FROM: _____

Quest Media Training, LLC
QuestMediaTraining.com
ZakiyaLarry.com

TABLE OF CONTENTS

LET'S START HERE

Welcome to *Master the Media, The Step-By-Step Guide to Elevating Your Brand On Air, On Camera and On Stage*.

This is now your go to step-by-step guide to elevate your brand on-air, on camera and on stage.

You have come to the right place whether you aim to elevate your brand or influence by appearing on various media platforms from TV, radio, or newspapers– to blogs, podcasts and online magazines.

Before we dive into the practical details of securing TV appearances, radio interviews, or newspaper features, we must lay the groundwork. This crucial step often gets overlooked, leading to missed opportunities. You see, it is not as simple as preparing a pitch or a press release and expecting media coverage to magically appear.

First, it is important to recognize that this information can be tailored to suit the unique needs of your business and vision. Regardless of where you currently stand in your career or business, rest assured that you will receive valuable information relevant to your situation.

As you go through this book, it is also important to take notes (and apply) as you will gain insights from the various action items carefully crafted to elevate your media preparedness.

1

Additionally, you are encouraged to engage on social media by posting your ah-ha moments with the hashtags #MasterTheMedia, #QuestMediaTraining, and #ZakiyaLarry, to show your accountability as you go through this book and the process.

This book will lay a foundation. However, if you would like to accelerate your results and work with the author, Zakiya Larry, on a one-on-one basis, she will help you uncover your current positioning and define your aspirations (and the strategy to get there) for your brand.

Media for your brand is possible, so this process is essential. Media professionals expect you to take charge and actively contribute to their content.

While entrepreneurs and business owners often think about what they can provide to their customers, Zakiya emphasizes the need to develop an entirely different mindset when it comes to engaging with the media and the public. This is the cornerstone of her coaching when she delves deeper with more personalized support.

You must learn to speak their language and operate in a manner that resonates with the masses, beyond just your target audience. It is crucial to analyze your brand from a broader perspective, considering how you can make it relevant to a wider audience.

So, if you truly aspire to *Master The Media*, it all begins with laying the groundwork. Take diligent notes, broaden your thinking, and contemplate how you can make your brand universally appealing.

Get ready to unlock the secrets of developing a media strategy that truly works for you in today's fast-paced world. In every field, from entrepreneurship to nonprofit leadership, media exposure is an absolute game-changer.

But how exactly can you harness its power?

How can you create a media strategy that catapults your message to the masses?
Welcome to this definitive guidebook, where you will be equipped with essential tips and tools to craft a media strategy tailored to your unique goals and target audience.

Together, we will embark on a journey that starts with understanding the media industry, then a deep analysis of your brand, your company, and your goals.

What do you truly want to achieve?

Do you aspire to be featured in top business publications or connect with a specific demographic like women or families?

By setting a clear goal for yourself, we can then delve into how to identify and engage those key individuals through the power of (FREE) media.

Within these pages is Zakiya's experience as a Global Chief of Communications and agency founder who specializes in strategy, training, media, and crisis, with a diverse range of clients around the world.

She took the time to assess her goals, client list, and her role as a public relations/strategic communications expert to determine the segment of people she wanted to reach. Zakiya then reached into her nearly two-decades of experience that started in the newsrooms of radio and TV stations, to share best-practices with her favorite demographic– you.

Currently, her target audience consists of entrepreneurs and corporate leaders seeking broader media interest to drive impact, or personal elevation. She also has a deep respect for individuals who are passionate about important issues. Having this focus enables her to connect with and serve these specific groups more effectively.

Remember, before we delve into the strategies for achieving media success, its crucial to lay the groundwork that will get you there and ensure you stay there.
The importance of groundwork cannot be stressed enough, and it must be done long before you even qualify for a media appearance.

Here at Quest Media Training, we offer the opportunity to work closely with our experienced coaches, investing several hours to uncover the essence of who you are and where you aspire to go. This process is vital because you need absolute clarity on your identity and the unique value you bring to the general public.

As an entrepreneur or business leader, you have likely contemplated what you can offer your customers, and that is commendable. However, when you work through this guide, you will revolutionize your thinking and expand your perspective on connecting with the wider public. You will also learn how to make your identity and message truly relevant to them. This is where our expertise shines.

In the upcoming chapters, we will delve into various aspects that resonate with audiences beyond your brand.

We will analyze your strengths, weaknesses, opportunities, and threats, uncovering strategic ways to leverage them to your advantage.

You will also gain invaluable insights into creating a compelling media kit, crafting persuasive pitches, and acing media interviews with finesse.

By the time you reach the final pages of this book, you will possess the skills and unwavering confidence to develop a media strategy that not only works but propels you towards your goals.

Are you ready to embark on this transformative journey? Let us dive in and unlock the secrets to a media strategy that sets you apart from the competition.

CHAPTER 1 - WHAT CAN MEDIA DO FOR MY BRAND?

First, Understand Media and Media Relations

It is universally understood that customer relations is relating to one's customers. It is easy to understand that business relations is defined as the connections that exist between all entities that engage in commerce.

Public relations follows a similar structure in definition, but quickly becomes misinterpreted. Public relations is NOT marketing, copywriting, brand design or even media placements. These elements are tools within public relations. Marketing runs on a parallel course and creates a mutually beneficial relationship with PR efforts. Public relations is reputation building, shaping perception, driving trust and buy in. A tactic, or tool to accomplish this within PR is media relations— the reason you picked up this book.

1. *What Is Media Relations?*

Media relations boosts visibility through earned media (visibility for free,) vs. paying for an ad or airtime, which is

7

marketing. Media relations involves strategy, storytelling, relationships, and creativity.

To effectively navigate the realm of media relations, it is essential to have a solid understanding of what media encompasses and how it operates.

2. *What Is Media?*

Media refers to various channels of communication that facilitate the dissemination of information to a wide audience.

In today's interconnected world, media plays a vital role in shaping public opinion, influencing consumer behavior, and creating brand awareness.

Credentialed professionals consider media to be sources based on objective reporting, balanced coverage and fact sharing only.

This includes traditional news outlets such as:
- Newspapers
- Magazines
- Television
- Radio

Media has now expanded to digital platforms like:
- Websites
- Online magazines
- Online news publications and station websites

The newer, most prolific frontier includes:
- Social media
- Podcasts
- Blogs

This newer frontier blurs the lines of opinion and objectivity. The untrained eye would consider media contributors to be journalists, though there are different training levels, codes of conduct, and ethics to which journalists must adhere. This is important to note as the media platform you choose for your brand affects how your brand is positioned and perceived. It is not just about views if your aim is to build credibility and grow your bottom line.

Understanding the media landscape involves familiarizing yourself with different types of media outlets, their target audiences, editorial guidelines, and the formats they typically use to present information.

Traditional media outlets, such as newspapers and magazines, often have established credibility and reach a broad audience. Television and radio provide audiovisual platforms that can convey your message effectively, while digital media platforms offer a vast array of options for engaging with audiences, including interactive content, multimedia presentations, and direct audience interaction.

3. The Importance of Media Relations

Media relations is the strategic practice of managing relationships between an organization or individual and the media.

Building positive media relationships is crucial for businesses and brands as it allows them to amplify their messages, reach a broader audience, and establish credibility and trust. Effective media relations can help shape public perception, enhance brand reputation, and contribute to overall business success.

By proactively engaging with the media, organizations can gain valuable exposure, attract potential customers or clients, and position themselves as thought leaders in their respective industries. Engaging with the media also provides an opportunity to address any misconceptions or respond to negative coverage, allowing you to maintain control over the narrative surrounding your brand.

However, media relations require a delicate balance of transparency and strategic messaging. It is important to build genuine relationships with journalists and reporters based on trust, respect, and open communication. By nurturing these relationships, you can increase the likelihood of media coverage and establish yourself as a reliable source of information within your industry.

Media: Their Role Vs. Your Goal

Before diving into media relations, it is crucial to grasp the role of the media.

In today's information-driven society, the media serves as a vital intermediary between events and the public, playing a significant role in shaping public opinion, influencing societal narratives, and fostering democratic discourse.

While their primary goal is to inform and educate their audience, the media also faces the constant challenge of attracting viewers or readers to sustain their business operations in an increasingly competitive landscape.

At its core, the media serves as a conduit of information, seeking to provide timely, accurate, and relevant news stories, features, and analyses.

By presenting a diverse range of perspectives and voices, they aim to present a comprehensive picture of events unfolding locally, nationally, and globally.

Through investigative journalism, the media uncovers hidden truths, exposes corruption, and holds those in power accountable for their actions. Moreover, by shedding light on underreported issues and marginalized communities, the media plays a critical role in promoting social justice and equality.

However, it is important to recognize that the media operates within a commercial framework, relying on advertising revenue and audience engagement to sustain their operations.

In today's age of digital media, where attention spans are shorter and competition for viewership is intense, media outlets must navigate a delicate balancing act between delivering substantive content and satisfying audience demand for captivating and entertaining stories.

As a public relations professional or someone seeking media coverage, understanding the media's dual nature is essential. By providing valuable content that benefits their audience, you increase your chances of securing coverage. Journalists and media professionals are constantly searching for engaging, informative, and relevant stories that resonate with *their* readers or viewers, not necessarily your customer base or target audience.

Therefore, by crafting your message in a way that aligns with their objectives, you not only increase the likelihood of media attention but also contribute to the overall quality and integrity of the news landscape.

Building strong relationships with journalists and understanding their needs can also enhance your media relations efforts. Recognizing the pressures they face, such as tight deadlines and limited resources, and providing them with well-researched information, access to knowledgeable sources, and compelling story angles can greatly facilitate their work.

As I like to say to my team and consulting clients; "Do the producers' work for them."

Quick Story Time:

One of my clients was embarking upon a book tour that I believed could command national media attention. I analyzed the audiences and content using the same tips I share in this book and decided to pitch (the leading American syndicated daytime television talk show at that time) The Dr. Oz Show.

Having been a producer in TV and radio news, I knew the challenges of building multiple segments, day after day. Instead of sending a pitch and crossing my fingers, I decided to do something bold. I instead designed the entire segment, from the flow of the conversation to the questions that would be asked, to on-set examples, and even down to pre- and post-show audience engagement. Then, I included a sample script. I rounded out this approach with links to my client's previous on-air appearances for performance and delivery reference. I clicked 'send' and waited.

Soon after I sent the e-mail, the producer quickly booked my client, thanking me multiple times in the process. When we arrived at the New York studio, I was excited for the rehearsal and walkthrough. As I approached the host, Dr. Oz, to shake his hand and formally introduce my client, I caught a glimpse of the famous note cards in his hand. That day, the cards were beyond famous, but familiar.

*The words on the cards were not mere notes for the conversation between Dr. Oz and my client. The words were a **copy and paste** from the concept and script that I sent to the producer. I was elated. This meant that my practice of "Do the producer's work for them," was proven. This also meant that my client was incredibly prepared because the content I sent over was from my client's positioning and zone of genius, curated for a wider audience. This was not the first or last time my method paid off, but it was the most direct adoption of my content.*

Part of the success of a similar symbiotic method is in the vetting of the media outlet and how a pitch is crafted. We will explore and shore up your vetting and pitching a bit later.

By positioning yourself as a reliable and valuable resource, you not only increase your chances of securing media coverage but also foster long-term partnerships that benefit both parties.

Just know that understanding the multifaceted role of media is essential for effective media relations. While their primary goal is to inform and educate their audience, media outlets also operate within a competitive industry where capturing and retaining audience attention is crucial.

By recognizing this dynamic and providing valuable content that benefits *their* audience, you can increase the likelihood of securing media coverage while contributing to the overall quality and impact of the news landscape.

CHAPTER 2 - WHAT DO I NEED TO MASTER THE MEDIA?

If you want to gain media coverage for your business, organization, or personal brand, taking an honest assessment of your brand is essential. Start by asking yourself, "Am I media-ready?"

The answer to the question is a resounding 'yes' once you have gathered all the elements needed to master the media.

In overview form, those key elements are:

- A clear personal/organizational/business brand
- A story angle that connects to a headline or current event
- A solid pitch for producers
- A media kit (this will also be useful for on-stage opportunities)

Now let's go deeper and walk through exactly how to craft each of those elements for you in a way that positions you for media success and brand elevation.

1. A Clear Brand

You may have been taught that a brand is what other people say about your company, product, or service. Another school of thought is that a brand is how you show up online, or the logo, or website and colors.

To truly master the media, you must master your message. To do that you must master this elusive yet popular word, brand.

I have been asserting for more than a decade and will continue as long as I practice strategic communications that a brand is none of the popular external factors previously mentioned.

A logo, a website, and the elements in between are simply expressions of a brand. Taught starting in 2011, stated publicly in a viral social media video in 2016 and here again today I assert that – **your brand is your promise.**

Take a moment to dive into these next brand-defining steps by answering the following questions:

- What is the promise of you?
- What will people or customers experience every time they interact with you?

_____

_____

_____

_____

Now, interaction can be online, on social media, in person or on your website, where the external brand elements start to take residence. This is now an illuminated full circle view of consistent, effective branding. Define your brand promise first then unpack how your products or services are a reflection or illustration of that promise, finally choose how to best communicate these findings in a visual manner.

Finally, here is a business elevation hack:
If you define your brand as a promise, you then open nearly endless possibilities for products, services, and ways you can express this brand.

You have just discovered the quickest way to brand longevity and how to diversify your income while maintaining brand congruence.

2. *A Story Angle That Connects To A Headline Or Current Event*

Now that you are clear on your promise, or your brand, examine your expertise and products. Next, think about what conversations are happening across the various forms of media to which you would add value, based on your promise.

For example:
I promise to provide strategy, visibility, and a way out of crisis for top-performing brands and executive leadership.

On the national media landscape, there are often large companies that run into a PR misstep. There are always celebrities who slip up and have a public crisis. It just so happens that one of the ways I deliver on my promise is through PR and crisis mitigation services.

With this in mind, when breaking news or hot topics occur, reporters call me as their go-to expert. Years ago, I or my team would pitch reporters who were covering the topics of missteps. The pitch outlined my experience, value... my promise, as it relates to being able to offer insight and new perspective on that headline of the day. The time of year or state of a product in my business did not matter. My pitch and topics were evergreen.

Evergreen topics are ones that do not expire when the seasons change. In the above example, a PR misstep can happen at any time. I did not limit my topic to slip ups with inclusive holiday toys, or back to school content. While these are great angles for when those seasons arrive, having evergreen topics increase your chances for ongoing media exposure and the benefits that come with it.

Create your evergreen pitch topics.
What issues do you solve, conversation can you lead, or perspective can you add for the everyday person, no matter the time of the year?

_____

_____

_____

3. A Solid Pitch For Producers

Let's dissect the ideal pitch.
Since you are here to master the media, you are likely aware of the target audience for your business or brand. In this section, we will expand your thinking and reach by adding a target audience for media coverage.

Step 1: Take the media outlet's target audience into consideration. A secret PR tip is that this can usually be found on an outlet's website, buried at the bottom in tiny print. Look for 'Contact Us' and follow the trail to the advertising kit.   Within their advertising kit will be a breakdown of their viewership demographics. Many years ago, this information was readily available on a homepage, but now it takes a bit of digging.

Quick Story Time:

When I produced in a TV newsroom, we had a mock viewer profile. Her photo and stats were printed on a sheet of paper and hung on the wall at every desk. Her name was 'Sally,' aged between 40-55, was a female, married, mom and white. We knew to take this into consideration when writing and choosing stories. This did not limit or skew our coverage but informed us who was watching and what they needed.

Every outlet has a viewership profile. Feel free to use this one as a start.

An additional approach is to choose a reporter who covers the topics you wish to address. This way, you bypass the audience vetting for established interest in the subject matter. The audience approach model is people focused; this second approach is topic focused.

Step 2: Determine your goals for landing this media opportunity.

Who are you trying to reach? Is it a specific demographic or industry? What do you want them to know, or do once you have their attention?

Once you have identified your target audience and goals, research the relevant media outlets and journalists who cover that topic.

Create a comprehensive list of journalists and media outlets that you want to target. Make sure to include their contact information, such as email addresses and phone numbers. You can also utilize social media platforms like X (Twitter) and LinkedIn to connect with journalists. Often, journalists have their email addresses in their bios on X. Another secret PR gem to hold.

Step 3: Craft your pitch. Keep in mind that journalists receive numerous pitches every day, so it is crucial to make yours stand out. Begin with a strong subject line that succinctly summarizes your story. Your pitch should be concise, focusing on the most significant aspects of your story. Keep it short.

Personalize your pitch for each journalist and media outlet. Explain why you believe their audience would find your story interesting and how it aligns with their beat or area of coverage.

Also include your media kit in your pitch, making it easy for journalists to access them. You can provide links to your website or attach PDF files to your email. Make sure these materials include examples of you speaking in another press interview if possible. Journalists want to know that you can perform well on camera.

Persistence is key but remember to strike a balance. Follow up with journalists after a few days but avoid bombarding them with excessive emails or phone calls. If they do not respond after a few follow-ups, move on to the next journalist on your list.

Keep in mind that gaining media coverage takes time and effort, but it can be a valuable tool for increasing your visibility and credibility. Continuously refine your pitch strategy and cultivate relationships with journalists and media outlets.

In conclusion, developing a strong media kit, combined with a well-crafted pitch and pitch strategy, are essential for obtaining media coverage. By following these steps and tips, you can enhance your chances of getting your story in front of the right people and elevating your brand.

Start your evergreen pitch draft now.

Subject Line: Expert on Breaking News (replace with specific topic)

Hello (reporter's name),

I noticed you recently covered (insert current event). **Great piece. A fresh angle to discuss with your audience is** (your perspective). **I am** (your name and title that includes your brand) **and am available to** (give tips, share recipes with a live cooking demo, share expert perspective).

This would both enlighten and entertain your audience because (give clear reason).

My perspective is based on (your experience, brief bio, or skillset. Example: my 15 year experience as an insulated cup designer).

I am available as early as (give dates that are within the same week you send the email). **What is your interest and next availability for me/my client** (give client's name) **to interview with you?**

Feel free to contact me directly at (add contact information and a friendly email close out.)

Notice that selling a product, book or service was never mentioned. Media's job is to inform, not sell.
To gain access to their platform for free you must add to informing their audience. The trick is to elegantly mention your brand as part of your expertise, not as something to sell.

4. A Media Kit

Having a comprehensive media kit will set you apart. A media kit is a package of information about you, your business, or your organization that you can share with the media to capture their interest in covering your story. A media kit is also always requested by event planners looking for speakers.

But what exactly goes into a comprehensive media kit?

In this section, we will break down each piece of the puzzle, empowering you to create a polished, professional, and effective package that catches the eye of producers, reporters, and other members of the media.

Step 1: The Anchor

The first piece of the media kit puzzle is the content that anchors the entire kit.
While a media kit can include flashy graphics, clickable links, and embedded videos, the most crucial element is the content itself.

You do not necessarily need to focus on high-level design with fancy visuals. Often, a well-crafted media kit created in Microsoft Word and saved as a PDF can be just as effective. Remember, it is the content that draws people in, not necessarily the design.

When it comes to media, you will need a bio that is concise and specific to who you are and what you do. While many bios traditionally start with the date of birth, this information is often unnecessary and can be off-putting to media professionals. Instead, be direct and to-the-point.

For example, if you are a nonprofit founder with a remarkable track record of empowering women and children since 1972, emphasize those accomplishments and the value you bring.

Step 2: Photos and Logo

The next step in creating a comprehensive media kit is to include high-quality photos and your logo.

Media professionals often find it frustrating when they have to request specific photos or images. To streamline the process, proactively provide a current, high-resolution headshot and a separate file containing your logo.

By having these visual elements readily available, you empower producers to incorporate your photos and logo seamlessly into their graphics and visuals. This contributes significantly to the PR value you bring and helps you stand out in the media landscape.

Step 3: Audience and Topics

The third is to consider your target audience and the topics you can address. Much of this work has been done with your evergreen pitch, illustrating how efficient this system can be once you understand it.

Now, this is where the umbrella concept, or overarching topics, come into play. You can create a heading like "April is available to speak on the following topics:" followed by a breakdown of four different subjects you can address.

Take some time to brainstorm and jot down 3-5 key topics you can address:

1._____

_____

_____

_____

2._____

_____

_____

_____

3._____

_____

_____

_____

4._____

_____

_____

_____

_____

5._____

_____

_____

_____

_____

When defining your target audience, aim for a balance between specificity and broad appeal. Use one or two-word descriptors like "parents," "movie lovers," or "children" to reach a broader audience. Strive for a balance that allows producers to understand who you are, what you offer, and whether you would make compelling television.

This robust chapter just walked you through years of training, months of working with a publicist and thousands of dollars' worth of techniques, secrets, and tools.

Put it all together as soon as possible and get ready to elevate.

CHAPTER 3 - HOW TO REACH OUT TO MEDIA

Now that you have crafted an expert media approach and unique evergreen angles, it is time to take the next and ultimate step and connect with various media outlets.

The last step is the pitch process, where the real work begins.
With pitching, the work does not end with sending the initial email.

While we have delved into crafting the ideal pitch, how to find contact information for journalists and best practices, the pitch process is a delicate one. We will now focus on it and go deeper.

In this chapter, we will delve into the strategies and techniques that will help you build rapport with journalists, create lasting relationships, and increase your chances of securing future media coverage. Understanding their preferences, needs, and deadlines will enable you to tailor your approach and increase the likelihood of becoming a media master.

You will also learn about 'vetting' as promised earlier in this guide.

It is time to take proactive, strategic steps in reaching out to media contacts and offering your story.

Vetting Media Opportunities

When seeking media opportunities, it is important to keep in mind that not all coverage is equal. Quality is more important than quantity. Targeting outlets with a strong reputation and engaged audience can yield better results than aiming for broad but less influential coverage.

Before agreeing to an interview or article, it is crucial to conduct thorough research on both the outlet and the journalist involved. Consider the journalist's background and expertise in the subject matter. Review their previous work to gauge professionalism, knowledge, and their ability to provide fair and unbiased coverage. Seek out journalists who have covered similar topics or industries in the past, as their experience and understanding will lend credibility to your story. By positioning yourself with journalists who have a genuine interest in your message, you increase the likelihood of receiving accurate and comprehensive coverage.

Also, vet or research the outlet. Seek out reputable media outlets with a substantial reach and a track record of delivering high-quality content.

Look for outlets known for their journalistic integrity, accuracy, and ethical reporting practices. Reputable outlets not only enhance your brand's or organization's reputation, but also ensure that your message reaches a wider and more discerning audience.

While reach is important, it is equally crucial to assess the relevance of the media outlet's audience to your objectives. Targeting outlets that cater to your target demographic or industry ensures that your message will resonate with the right audience. A smaller outlet with a niche readership can sometimes be more impactful than a larger outlet with a broader, but less relevant, audience.

Example: You own an HR company, and your life-long dream is to be on Good Morning America. While that experience would feed your ego and make you the talk of the PTA, the audience is not looking to engage with you. A profile piece in the Society for Human Resource Management (SHRM) newsletter would boost your credibility and could create warm leads for your business. This is the impact of strategic media coverage, even if your mom and carpool lane buddies will not see it while getting dressed in the morning. Your ideal clients and bank account will notice.

In summary, not all media opportunities hold the same value, necessitating a thorough evaluation process– or vetting. Carefully researching the media outlet and journalist, seeking reputable outlets with a strategic reach, and ensuring alignment with your message and objectives are key to making informed decisions about media engagements. By strategically selecting the right media opportunities and the ideal journalist to handle your story, you can maximize the impact of your message and effectively reach your target audience.

Crafting Your Message

Once you have identified potential media opportunities, it is crucial to develop a compelling and concise message that aligns with your goals and resonates with your target audience. Your message should clearly communicate your unique value proposition, key differentiators, and the benefits your business or brand offers.

Crafting a media-friendly message involves distilling complex information into easily digestible sound bites or quotable statements. This will help journalists and reporters capture your key points accurately and effectively in their coverage. It is important to remember that media professionals often work under tight deadlines and face information overload, so providing them with concise and compelling messages increases the likelihood of your story being picked up and shared.

Tailoring your content to the specific audience of each media outlet is crucial for success. Research each outlet's audience demographics, interests, and editorial tone. This information will help you adapt your message to align with their expectations and resonate with their readers or viewers. By speaking directly to their concerns and addressing topics that are relevant to them, you increase the chances of your content being well-received and generating meaningful engagement.

Aim to **provide value** to the audience by sharing insights, expertise, or solutions to their problems. By positioning yourself as a trusted authority in your field, you can establish credibility and build long-term relationships with both the media and your target audience.

When crafting your message, remember to strike a balance between being informative (for them) and promotional (for you). While it is important to promote your brand or business, overtly sales-driven content may be met with skepticism by the audience and the media alike. It will certainly ensure that you will not be invited back.

Following Up Strategically

Earlier in the guide, you were taught how to find reporters, vet them, and reach out to them, all anchored in strategy.

Following up is a crucial step in the media outreach process. Follow up must be strategic, ensuring that you stay on their radar without becoming a nuisance. Building rapport through strategic follow-ups will help nurture relationships and potentially lead to future media opportunities.

Be timely and persistent with follow-ups, without being pushy or intrusive. Offer support rather than push for their time and attention.

The news cycle turns over in less than 24 hours, so sending check in emails or asking if there is any other information you can provide in the morning and before 4p in your time zone, keeps you on their radar. These are windows that I've found works for me in my practice. Be fluid based on the reporters' needs and responsiveness.

Sometimes the reporter likes your content but does not have the bandwidth to take on your story at the time. Silence is not always a 'no.' I recommend starting with a follow-up cadence of three times over the course of a week. Within this time period, you may see the headlines shift, so you are able to update or enhance your pitch in real time if needed.

Be Available and Responsive:
Media professionals often work on tight deadlines, and their schedules can be unpredictable. To build trust and maintain good relationships, you must be available and responsive when they reach out to you.

Timely responses to their inquiries, requests for additional information, or interview opportunities demonstrate your professionalism and commitment. By being dependable and accommodating, you will establish yourself as a valuable resource and increase your chances of being featured in their stories.

Example: I have booked national media opportunities for executives who then requested to take a week to discuss it with colleagues who lack press expertise. The opportunity, of course, expired. The teams were then disappointed and pressed for another opportunity. Remember the insight into news cycles, the reporters' overwhelm and being timely and relevant? Leaders, are you stalling your elevation and undermining your comms team's expertise by measuring it against your assumptions?

Nurture Long-Term Relationships:
Building lasting relationships with media contacts can open doors to future opportunities. Cultivating genuine connections based on mutual respect and collaboration will position you as a trusted source and increase the likelihood of future media coverage.

Contact the reporter and congratulate them when they publish a new article or win an award, even if you are not involved. Do not ask for anything or pitch. Build the connection. This is still part of follow up because not every pitch will be picked up every time, but you want to environment to be primed for next time.

Embrace Feedback and Continuous Improvement:
Receiving feedback from media professionals is an invaluable opportunity for growth and improvement. Welcome feedback with an open mind and use it to refine your media outreach strategies. Actively seek feedback after they have covered your story or especially when they have declined a pitch.

Use the input to adjust your approach or pitch. By embracing feedback and continuously improving your media outreach efforts, you will enhance your chances of securing future media coverage.

Collaborate on Exclusive Content:
Building strong relationships with media contacts can lead to collaborative opportunities for creating exclusive content. Collaborative content not only strengthens your relationship with journalists and producers but also increases the likelihood of receiving favorable coverage. An example of pitching exclusive content ideas was included in my *The Dr. Oz Show* story time. The key is to offer something to one outlet only and assuring them that their coverage will be the first and only with a particular angel. Work closely with media contacts to develop these kinds of compelling stories.

Remember to Express Gratitude:
Always thank the journalists and outlets that provided your coverage. Reach out to them individually to thank them for the opportunity and express your appreciation for their support and hard work. This helps foster positive relationships and may lead to future collaborations or follow-up stories.

Reaching out to media contacts requires a strategic and thoughtful approach. Embrace feedback, continuously improve your strategies, and explore collaborative opportunities to expand your reach.

With these strategies in place, you will navigate the media with confidence and effectively share your story with the world.

CHAPTER 4 - HOW CAN I STAND OUT?

In today's competitive media landscape, it is essential to find ways to distinguish your brand.

Your story deserves to be heard, so in this chapter, we will explore strategies to help you pinpoint the top three key differentiators that set your organization apart from others in your industry. We will then delve into the process of crafting grab-worthy content to help you become the preferred thought leader, and secure media hits when multiple pitches of the same topic are on a journalist's desk.

Leverage Media Training and Events:
Media training workshops and industry events offer valuable networking opportunities and insights into the media landscape. Media training programs, like the ones uniquely designed by Quest Media Training, help you to refine your interview skills, learn how to effectively communicate your uniqueness, and build confidence in front of the camera.

Media training, when done well by a professional who keeps crisis mitigation and reputation management in mind, also equips you to speak on your toes, nearly control the follow up questions the reporter asks, and teaches you how to tell your story within a confined timeframe without rushing or omitting key details.

Additionally, some media brands host virtual and in-person events. The topics range from finance, diversity, equity and inclusion, community building and more. Check a network's website to get involved. The journalists are always the speakers and moderators at these events, so this is an ideal way to connect with media professionals face-to-face and establish personal connections.

Prepare for Media Interviews:
Securing media interviews is exciting, but preparation before the big day makes you a standout success. Practice possible questions the journalist may ask. As a communications executive, I circumvent the blind question process for my clients. But for the sake of your personal journey, draft five to ten questions you may be asked, based on your pitch.

Next, practice answering the questions with a trusted partner who will also give you honest feedback.

Draft talking points that are pulled directly from your pitch, mission, story and goal. Get familiar with these points and guide the conversation back to them at every opportunity. Now there are nuances and techniques that must be taught by an experienced media coach but understand that these points should be used as answers to any question. This technique not only helps you to manage nerves because of familiarity with the content, but it is brand elevating. The new audience will hear your brand points exactly the way you intend them to be delivered.

Research Your Competitors:

As part of your interview prep, research and understand your competitors who are gaining media attention. How are they speaking about their brand in relation to the conversation?

How are they positioning themselves in the media? With this in mind, begin to differentiate yourself.

Use your findings to identify gaps in conversation and even in the market. Try to identify three points of differentiation and weave those into your talking points without ever mentioning your competitors. As you elevate in your media appearances, these same findings and points can (and should) be incorporated into your pitches.

Monitor Industry Trends and Adapt:
A close second to researching your competitors, to maintain your competitive edge, it is essential to stay informed about industry trends and adapt accordingly. Keep a close eye on emerging technologies, shifts in consumer preferences, and changes in the media landscape. By staying ahead of the curve, you can identify new opportunities to pitch your unique qualities and adjust your messaging to align with current headlines.

Tailor Your Content to Build Audience Trust:
Once you have identified your key differentiators and developed strong talking points, it is essential to tailor your content to create audience buy-in of your brand or message. People buy from those they know, like and trust. They will also defend them should a crisis arise.

Include true compelling stories or personal anecdotes and reference case studies that demonstrate your promise in real-life scenarios. These narratives should resonate with media professionals, their audience, and your target audience, alike. This technique will highlight the value and positive impact of your brand in a memorable way.

Leverage Data and Metrics:
To further strengthen your position as an expert or thought leader, leverage data and metrics to support your claims. Quantify the impact and results your organization or brand has achieved using concrete numbers and statistics. This data-driven approach adds credibility and demonstrates the effectiveness of your organization's differentiators.

Incorporate Visual and Multimedia Elements:
In today's digital age, visual and multimedia elements play a vital role in capturing attention and conveying information effectively. If you are savvy and ready to jump ahead, offer to enhance your interview by creating and incorporating engaging visuals such as infographics, charts, or videos that highlight your talking points.

When I practiced as a publicist, I often created charts and visuals for client interviews, and they were always well received. Simply clear the idea with the journalist, first. Many will excitedly accept the offer. Others will love the idea and have their team create the graphics, based on your directions and model. Either way, you have just elevated your interview because visual storytelling has the power to leave a lasting impression.

Leverage Social Media Platforms:

Social media platforms provide an excellent opportunity to amplify your unique qualities and engage with a broader audience. Develop a strong social media presence that showcases your organization's differentiators through compelling content, thought-provoking discussions, and interaction with followers. Utilize platforms like X(Twitter,) LinkedIn, Facebook, or Instagram to share your expertise, highlight success stories, and cultivate relationships with media professionals.

Continuously Evaluate and Refine:

Differentiation is an ongoing process, and it is crucial to continuously evaluate and refine your approach. Regularly assess the effectiveness of your messaging and the impact of your unique qualities on media coverage. Monitor feedback from journalists, producers, and your target audience to understand how well your content and pitches resonate with them. Use this feedback to refine your communication strategy and make necessary adjustments to maximize your media impact.

Remember that consistency, creativity, and adaptability are key to capturing media attention and building a powerful reputation. Embrace the opportunities that arise, continually refine your messaging, and showcase your distinct qualities to make a lasting impression on journalists, producers, and your target audience.

By implementing these strategies and consistently focusing on succinct storytelling that adds value, you or your brand will stand out in the media landscape.

What ideas to stand out has this chapter inspired? Capture them here:

_____

_____

_____

_____

_____

_____

_____

_____

_____

_____

_____

_____

_____

CHAPTER 5 - WHAT IF I DON'T HAVE A STORY TO TELL?

This chapter will be the shortest one in this guide.

This question is asked across industries and experiences. Layoffs of communications teams happen because executive leadership assumes the answer.

To address this question in no uncertain terms;
You always have a story to tell.

Master the Media intentionally opened with insight into media vs. marketing and how storytelling plays a centric role in elevating your brand, impact, and bottom line.

No matter how seasoned a leader or entrepreneur may be, there is often (an unadmitted) novice when it comes to strategic communications. This is paired with assumptions. Some leaders believe that the absence of awards or new clients to announce means there is no story, so the brand does not need strategic communications.

This guide has been intentional in helping you to avoid this pitfall before reaching this chapter. Remember, watch the headlines and external conversations. Align your expertise. Life and industry create the story for you. Strategically pick it up and make magic for your brand.

You always have a story because life is always happening around us.

CHAPTER 6 - HOW TO CRAFT MY STORY?

By now, you may have realized how each chapter builds upon the last. You may have even noticed that you have already started groundwork for items that come full circle in a more significant way, later.

This is intentional. Your *Master The Media* guide is not only comprehensive as a reference tool but aims to be an efficient experience and short cut to media mastery for your brand.

We have explored the ins and outs of the industry and the way to a journalist's heart. You most recently learned how to create (relevant and useful) stories *seemingly* out of thin air.

Now it is time to create your personal story– or your Core Story. I call it your Core Story because it is at the center (core) of your message and holds the heart or mission of your brand.

In previous chapters, we reviewed anecdotes to be used on-air. Those are short and used to establish likeability and credibility.

Your Core Story drives a larger goal and creates connection with an audience. Your Core Story is especially useful on-camera and on-stage. Let's unpack how to create yours.

Establish a Clear Purpose:

To craft an effective Core Story, first define its purpose. Do you want to introduce your mission and values? Highlight key achievements or expertise? Empower a group? Sell more products or services? Identifying the objectives will help you structure your Core Story and create a cohesive narrative.

Introduce The Heart of Your Brand:

The purpose for your Core Story becomes its compass. Craft the narrative in a way that illustrates and drives toward that purpose.

Your experiences are rich and the reasons for how you operate are varied. The challenge issued here is for you to pick only the elements that point toward the purpose of your story.

Example:

Emma, CEO of Porter Enterprises, wants to empower more women to aim for the c-suite and encourage more investors to support Porter Enterprises.

Her story includes: Grew up in a rural community. Pushed to gender-stereotyped service jobs and away from higher education. Helped her parents with her eight siblings while working her way through college. Worked as a call center operator and eventually a teacher. Porter Enterprises has grown to serve every continent and grosses millions of dollars in revenue a year.

For the sake of time and space, this example is quite abbreviated, as content of our Core Story has taken a lifetime to draft.

Now, remember Emma's goals. What in her story can illuminate those goals and make her Core Story a great connecting point?

_____

_____

_____

_____

_____

_____

_____

_____

_____

_____

Here is what Emma's Core Story could look like in first person:

*"You may know me as the CEO of Porter Enterprises.
But to farmers and families back home in that little rural town that raised me, I'm just Emma."*

*"I am the Emma that went from answering phones to answering questions from eager elementary school children, to answering a board of directors about our most recent stand-out quarter.
I'm just the Emma that proved that girls belong anywhere they set their minds to. I'm also the Emma that took a lifetime of lessons on consistency, creativity, team management and an honest day's work, and leveraged them into an enterprise that continues to grow– yielding a consistent return on investment for those who believe in our vision."*

"Afterall, I know a thing or two about planting good seeds and bringing in a harvest."

Note that there are interesting elements left out of Emma's Core Story. College for that little country girl was a big deal. It may be tempting to include everything that has a special place in your memory, but your Core Story is to create a special place for your *goals* in someone else's memory.

Did you also gather that with Emma's goals and structure, she can swap out details should her audience or goal shift?

If she is invited to speak to the National PTA, Emma can keep the same open and close. Then, instead of talking about the financial return on investment, speak to the investment needed in children, of which she is aware as a former educator. All this content already exists, and her story structure is evergreen.

The trick is to lay out your Core Story elements and keep them streamlined enough to switch out if the platform calls for it. Emma's story can easily be a storytime on social media to build community, or a **keynote speech** on stage for a target audience. Of course, she can insert this story into a media interview when asked about her passions.

As you begin to think about your own Core Story, below are some elements you may consider incorporating. All the prompts do not have to be used for your story to be effective:

Share a Compelling Narrative:
People connect with stories, so make sure to weave a compelling narrative throughout your Core Story. Share the story of how your organization was founded, the challenges you have overcome, and the vision that drives your work. Incorporate personal anecdotes or testimonials that demonstrate the positive impact your organization has had on individuals or communities.

Highlight Your Team's Expertise:
Your team members play a crucial role in the success of your brand. Perhaps dedicate a section of your Core Story to highlight their expertise. Provide brief bios or profiles for key staff members, highlighting their qualifications and areas of specialization. Even mentioning names and roles in relation to the impact of your work will garner confidence and respect from listeners, as you showcase both your relatable leadership and the capabilities within your organization.

Use Engaging Language:
When writing the content for your Core Story, use engaging and conversational language. Avoid overly technical terms that might alienate audiences. Instead, aim for a tone that is informative yet relatable. Connect with your audience on a personal level and experience improved reputation and buy-in.

Emotionally Engage with Your Audience:
It is important to evoke emotion in your storytelling. Emotion connects with your audience on a deeper level by tapping into their own emotions, experiences, values, and aspirations. By creating an emotional connection through your story, you will leave a lasting impact and inspire action from both the media and the wider public.

Showcase Achievements and Impact:
Highlight any notable achievements, success stories, or the impact you have made in your field. Use specific examples to demonstrate the tangible results of your work. This not only reinforces your credibility but also displays your organization's dedication to making a difference.

Incorporate Calls to Action:
Your Core Story purpose is set. Inviting the audience to take part in that purpose is a strategic action that could lead to notable results.

Include clear calls to action, such as encouraging them to learn more about your cause by visiting your website, sign up for your newsletter, or contacting you for collaboration opportunities. Always invite interaction, not customers or sales.

Periodically Evolve Your Story:
Though your structure and promise are evergreen, it is important to periodically evolve your story to remain relevant, and to connect with different audiences. Monitor industry trends, societal changes, media interests and audience preferences. Over time, you will learn to adapt and refine your story, ensuring that it remains fresh and maintains impact.

Keep it Concise:
While it is important to provide sufficient information about your brand, it is equally important to keep the content concise and easily digestible. Avoid excessive details.
Remember, value over volume.

It is your turn.
One of my favorite exercises to do with leaders is *The Z Method*, a process I developed to find their core, create key messaging, uncover their best Core Story, and often lead them to their personal and professional purpose.

You have the next best thing, my guide. Take a moment to think through the elements in this chapter for your brand. Now, draft your Core Story with your purpose/goal and the structure illustrated by Emma and Porter Enterprises in mind.

_____

_____

_____

_____

_____

_____

_____

_____

_____

_____

_____

_____

Tip For Those Who Like Steps:

Start by providing a concise and engaging overview of your brand. Clearly communicate your mission, core values, and the overarching goal of your work. Focus on conveying the unique aspects of your brand that set it apart. Highlight any notable accomplishments or recognitions to establish credibility and demonstrate impact.

CHAPTER 7 - CAN I MAKE MONEY FROM MEDIA?

Once you have successfully secured media coverage and are prepared to deliver, you may be excited to see your sales jump right after your interview wraps. The question of making money from media is a persistent one, and this chapter will demystify the revenue impact of media and share strategies to leverage each opportunity.

Can you make money from media appearances?
The answer is 'no,' but also 'yes.'

Unpacking the 'NO':
Reputable media outlets do not pay you for an interview.

Most outlets will not pay for your travel to their location. National, big studio shows are an exception, but with limits. They will not accommodate expenses for a plus one.

You may not directly sell on a traditional media platform unless you have paid for advertising.

You will also never be charged by reputable media to interview with them. Your currency is your expertise.
This is why it is called *earned media*.

Many brand leaders hope that media opportunities are a silver bullet for your revenue. Keep the purpose of media in mind. It is to inform and make aware. For brands, it increases visibility, credibility, and reach. These elements become your currency and the next section outlines how to spend it.

Getting to the 'YE$':
Media opportunities are to be leveraged to bolster a system that increases your revenue. Having an offer and a funnel for capturing leads is the best way to leverage media opportunities.

Include that critical call to action during your interview. Include your contact information, or if your aim is to make more sales, share the information for where the audience can go and be converted to warm leads for your brand.

Part of your plan may be a funnel that captures email addresses for a free download. Upsell from there.
Paid and free platforms for funnels that I have used to do this include plug ins with Bluehost, AWeber, Kajabi, and a

host of others that a quick tour of reviews on your favorite social media platform will point you to.

Another key way to leverage your media appearance to make money is to share your interview on social media. Tag the outlet for new eyes. Here you can directly sell.

Example:
To celebrate my story about arts and crafts on ZLTV today, I'm offering 15% off my seasonal arrangements for my followers and fellow ZLTV fans. Visit mywebsite.com and use my code THANKSZLTV. And like the code says, thanks ZLTV for the opportunity.

By doing so, you not only provide your audience with valuable information but also establish yourself as a trusted and credible source within your industry. Encourage your followers to engage with the content, fostering conversations and generating further interest. Journalists look for guests that can drive engagement, and this can help your chances for future bookings.

Reputation Building:
There is a proverb that says, "A good name is rather to be chosen than great riches..."
So, while there is not an immediate cause and effect between media coverage and revenue growth, there is certainly a straight line. In addition, the boost to your

brand's reputation and creation of a 'good name' is priceless.

To fully maximize having media exposure, be sure to request a link of your interview and:

Incorporate it into your website
Prominently displaying your media hit on your press or media page serves as a testament to your expertise and the trust you command from reputable sources.

Include excerpts in your marketing materials
Alignment with media illustrates influence and reach. Potential clients and customers often react favorably to good press coverage. Consider also including clips in your presentations to further boost your credibility.

Use it as a powerful pitching tool
Including recent coverage in your pitches and media kit will attract the attention of other media outlets, establishing that you are a trusted source and a thought leader. It also demonstrates the value you can bring to their audience, expanding your visibility and reach.

Measure and track results

As with any growth strategy within your brand or organization, it is essential to measure and track the results of your efforts. Establish metrics to help you evaluate the success of your media outreach such as: number of media mentions, audience reach, website traffic, number of emails captured, or social media engagement. By monitoring and analyzing these metrics, you can gauge the effectiveness of your strategy, identify areas for improvement, and adjust your approach accordingly.

By incorporating the recommendations in this chapter into your media relations strategy, you can effectively work with the media to enhance your brand, establish yourself as an authority in your field, connect with a broader audience, attract new opportunities, and propel the growth of your business.

What offers can you create or share to capture warm leads and eventually lead to revenue?

_____

_____

_____

_____

_____

_____

What type of funnel will you establish?

_____

_____

_____

_____

_____

What platform will you use?

_____

_____

_____

_____

_____

_____

_____

_____

_____

_____

_____

CHAPTER 8 - HOW TO SHINE WHEN ITS SHOW TIME

You have laid the groundwork, pitched strategically, booked the media interview, and practiced to get to this moment.

It is time to appear on a larger platform.

Each technique will close with a note about how that skill applies to each specific platform.

For the purposes of this guide, platforms are defined as:

On-Air
Any third-party-owned broadcast medium that captures and distributes your speaking, thought leadership, or content in an interview format to be consumed visually or audibly.

On-Camera
Recorded content without an additional participant conducting the interview. Examples include self-recorded videos, virtual presentations, keynotes, and online meetings.

67

On-Stage
Platforms are designed for primarily presenting before a live audience, even if cameras are present.

This chapter will guide you through the essential steps to ensure you are polished and make a strong impression once the lights are on and the camera is live. From preparedness to delivery and appearance, every aspect of your interview is crucial for communicating a professional brand and elevating your influence. Consider this chapter to be a media training masterclass in book form.

It Is What You Say AND How You Say It

Messaging That Connects
During the interview, maintaining focus and staying on message is vital. Answer questions honestly and concisely, referencing your key messages.

Pay attention to nonverbal cues and present yourself confidently and professionally, reflecting your expertise and credibility.

Tone and Voice Quality
Be mindful of your overall demeanor and tone during the interview. Speak naturally and project your voice only slightly above the level of your normal speaking voice to

communicate confidence and enthusiasm for the topic. Remember to speak clearly and enunciate, ensuring that your words are easily understood and resonate with the audience.

Listen to speakers and journalists you admire. Note how they modulate their voices, with levels in the sounds of the words they speak. Practice adding emphasis to words to avoid a monotone, dull delivery.

On-Air, On-Camera:
This section describes the ideal on-air delivery. The same techniques will help you to appear polished and professional on-camera as well.

On-Stage:
Practice similarly adding emphasis to words to avoid a monotone, dull delivery. However, there are more nuanced approaches for on-stage appearances that will be addressed in a later chapter.

Protect Your Brand, Control The Interview

Blocking and Bridging
This is an elite media coaching technique that may be a saving grace if you find yourself in a journalist's hot seat or are simply unprepared for a certain question.

Blocking and bridging is a method to deliver your core messaging without being derailed. The technique is to acknowledge the question asked but block where the reporter is going with that question, and bridge over to what you prefer to discuss.

Often, we see politicians use blocking and bridging, though many times, not very well.

Example:
A pre-election debate is live on primetime news.
The moderator opens the conversation and directs a question to the first candidate.
"Thank you so much for being here. Talk to us a little bit about how your first campaign stop went and what you're looking forward to next in Iowa."

Inevitably the candidate at the podium opens the response with something along the lines of; 'Hello, it is great to be here today. The people in Iowa are amazing. God bless America.'

Yet somehow within that same response, the aspiring elected official ends up talking about the price of oil and their plan to combat it. The moderator did not ask about oil prices.

What we observe in live action on a very regular basis is blocking and bridging. Block the initial question and bridge over to what your key messages and talking points.

The block is halting the current direction of a question.

The bridge is a statement of transition. It helps your mind to start to shift to that next subject matter and takes the listeners along with you.

Be cautious as this technique takes practice and a polished approach to avoid clunky responses that we see play out regularly in our election cycles. A poorly executed blocking and bridging attempt also shines a glaring, negative light on an attempt to avoid a question, leading to (spoken and unspoken) questions about transparency and authenticity.

Fortunately, our executive coaching clients turned media masters are not so obvious when they block and bridge because they employ the following elevated techniques:

1. To more smoothly 'block,' simply acknowledge that the question was asked, not the content of the question.

2. Make the bridge a positive and affirming statement. Making this a positive statement disarms the listener and creates more interest in your following statement.

3. Avoid refusal statements as a block method. This is one of the quickest ways to create your own PR crisis.

Long gone are the days when it is okay to say 'no comment' because we are now in an incredibly open, social media-driven society.

There is an expectation of insight into other's lives and thinking. "No comment" or a refusal to answer will back you into a corner every time.

Anything you want to discuss is possible with clear, appropriate, and strategic communications. You can shift the course of a conversation with just an effective bridge with a statement of transition that is not obvious but is certainly positive.

Adding humor will elevate you to an expert with this technique, especially when facing a negative question.

Quick Story Time:
I hold 13 pageant titles, gained across a 10-year span.

Not only did my pageant experience afford me opportunities to serve the community and make hundreds of appearances and speeches, but I was also able to graduate from college debt free and receive a generous refund check on my way out.

Scholarship pageants were an incredible training ground, and the prizes supplemented my full academic scholarships.

I continued to compete early into my professional career as a TV news journalist. Media interviews were par for the course as a titleholder, especially in my roles as Miss Texas Southern University, Miss Black Texas USA, and Miss Central Texas USA.

I remember a reporter from a major news outlet asked me a question that I hoped I would never hear;

"So, Zakiya. I understand that you're now a media coach, and public relations expert but I know that you've done pageants. Quite well might I add! Tell me, is there really fighting backstage? Do women really rip up each other's dresses? Oh my gosh!"

How limiting and stereotypical. Fortunately, I was a journalist and at that time, a new media coach. I was disappointed at the question, but prepared. I answered,

"(soft laughing) Hollywood has really done a number on pageants, huh?! I need to call somebody. Who do you know? (laughs)"

"Depictions really do drive perceptions. What I love about my pageantry experience, is that I'm now a depiction for young girls who wonder if they have to overthink their hobbies to be

considered serious and professional. I'm now a depiction of creativity and possibility for parents who wonder how they will send their child to college. My favorite is that I'm now a depiction for girls who look like me and have been told that they don't fit the beauty standard. There are millions of ways to be beautiful."

I take the responsibility of these depictions with me every day. I'm grateful for the confidence they infuse into what I do as a public relations director and now a new CEO of Quest Media Training.
I'm grateful for the journey and experiences."

What I did not say is: 'Well, I don't want to talk about the negativity and that's a stereotype of women fighting backstage. I would much rather talk about my company which is why you invited me here today.'

My bridge was affirmative, I used humor, and I took myself (and the journalist) on a journey to help my brain transition as I transitioned the conversation. The reporter asked me follow up questions about several points I shared in that one answer.

Over the years, I have observed in spoken conversations that the human mind more easily retains the first thing you say and the last thing you say. With my theory in mind, I observed countless interviews in the newsroom. I then tested this on myself in my many media interviews before teaching this idea to my clients.

It was settled.

For effective flow of conversation, particularly in a live interview, the last thing you say will often prompt or inspire the next question from the reporter. You have the agency and power to influence the direction of your interviews in a positive way.

As a warning and acknowledgement of reality, there may be hard news reporters that will drill down and circle back to their initial question asked before your block and bridge. While there are nuances and ways to rehearse that we work on in my coaching intensive, the most important thing for you to do is simply reiterate your block and bridge.

Ultimately, understand that blocking and bridging supports your interview and brand. It is an important technique that will set you apart.

On-Air, On-Camera and On-Stage:
Blocking and bridging applies to any platform or experience in which you are being asked questions. Use responsibly.

Talk in Soundbites

The industry term, soundbites, refers to a short piece of sound extracted from a recording, chosen because of how relevant to the story or memorable it is. In our social media era, think of it as a 'tweetable' – short, punchy, and sharable. Review your talking points and work to be able to deliver each point in under one minute. Mastering this technique forces you to deliver what is more important and increases your chances of having a sharable soundbite moment. Soundbites also help with attention spans and retention.

In interviews, it is about value, not volume. Most TV media interviews are less than three minutes long, so this technique will change the game for your brand. Features and podcasts offer significantly more time, but if you master this technique, you will be unstoppable on the longer form platforms.

Print interviews (anything written with no audio or video component)? Speaking in soundbites will help the journalist capture all your words as some still transcribe by hand. You will make their job easier, and your content has a higher likelihood of being printed in full and verbatim because interpretation and distillation was not left up to the overworked journalist. This is certainly a win-win.

On-Air, On-Camera:

This technique is an exact fit for on-air interviews. If your on-camera content is less than 5 minutes long, absolutely include soundbites to maximize your time and audience attention.

On-Stage:

Soundbites can be incorporated into a keynote or when speaking on a panel as a method to give the audience notes or create moments of impact. As a full delivery method, however, this technique is best used in full on-air and with select on-camera opportunities.

Now that we have learned how to protect your brand and control the interview with your messaging and voice, let us shift focus to what millions of people struggle with when doing camera work and public speaking– body language.

From nervous habits and odd movements to uncertainty about where to look or place your hands, this section will give you guidelines, techniques, and a boost of confidence.

Control Nervous Habits

How to Stop Saying 'Um'

From public speakers with eyes on the next level, to professionals facing a big presentation or even pageant competitors on a quest for the crown, eliminating 'um' becomes a worthy goal.

While this utterance may feel like a thorn in one's side, the good news is, 'um' is simply a space filler, allowing our brains more time to develop a thought or to catch up with our quick speaking. I noticed this consistently as a reporter and decided to develop a technique. I then used it as an interview coach and perfected it with many pageant contestants.

This common faux pas can be fixed in one simple step.
Step 1: Close your mouth.
That's it.

I coach my clients to literally close their mouths, teeth included, when they are searching for words or feel an 'um' coming on.

The mechanism of our mouths and word formation simply will not allow the sound if the teeth and lips are closed.

Challenge yourself right now. Say 'um.' The first few seconds of the sound, notice that your jaw is relaxed, and your mouth is slightly open. Now, begin to say 'um' again, but immediately close your teeth and lips. Keep those vocal cords going. This is now more difficult, correct? My proven technique is worth working into your daily conversations as practice.

When in an interview, closing your mouth to stop an 'um,' creates an opportunity to take a breath—a quick action that will help to get you back on track.

How to Stop Talking With Your Hands

The current media landscape looks for more authentic interaction, even if one is coached and polished. Years ago, I would have insisted that talking with one's hands must stop.

Now, my recommendation is to feel free to use your hands to emphasize points but avoid exaggerated movements. Be careful not to block your face with your movements or move so much that you create sound and feedback in the mic when doing so.

A good practice is to imagine you are holding a dinner plate with food on it. If you swing too far to either side, or lift too high up or too far down, you risk making a mess. Keep your arms and hands inside the frame of your body, with your elbows near your sides. When gesticulating, lift your hands no higher than you would if holding that plate.

On-Air, On-Camera and On-Stage:
This technique applies across platforms.

How to Sit, Best Way to Stand, Where to Look
If seated, sit up straight, but do not be rigid or stiff. Position yourself slightly forward in on the chair, near the edge of your seat, toward the interviewer. This posture allows your clothing to lay in a more flattering way and gives you a more streamlined appearance on-camera. It also communicates engagement with the reporter.

If standing, stand with your arms at the sides or one hand in pocket. Planting one foot slightly in front of the other will help you avoid swaying. Be mindful of and avoid obvious signs of discomfort or nervousness like foot tapping, clenched fists and shifting back and forth.

The reporter will usually tell you which camera will be recording if it is a multiple-camera shoot. However, **always** look directly at the reporter and never toward the camera, unless instructed to do so.

On-Air, On-Camera and On-Stage:
This technique applies across platforms.

On Camera Appearance

Wardrobe Dos and Don'ts

Consider your appearance and how you will represent yourself and your brand. Research the outlet that will be interviewing you to inform you of the culture of the audience and newsroom. Some call for more casual but polished attire. Others are quite buttoned up.

Dos

- Do strike a balance between your personal style and the culture of the media outlet. Note: dress for traditional newsrooms is usually business casual.

- Do wear mid-weight or layered clothing as it is the most comfortable choice. Most studios are cold until the lights are turned on, then become quite warm.

- If you have contact lenses, wear them instead of your glasses to avoid reflections and glare from the lights. If you do wear glasses, non-reflective lenses are preferable.

- Do accept makeup if offered, no matter your gender. Studios often offer powder to help avoid a shiny face or 'hot spots' on the face when on camera.

- If you apply your own makeup, do apply a matte finish to avoid shine. Apply blush and eye makeup slightly heavier than normal to avoid looking washed out under the lights.

Don'ts

• Don't wear busy or small patterns, they sometimes look distorted on camera. Solid bright colors look wonderful on camera, and do not clash with studio backgrounds.

• Don't wear solid white. It can cast unflattering light on the face and causes problems for TV cameras. It can sometimes cause issues lighting you and the environment, as all white can cast a glow.

• Don't wear large, shiny, or noisy jewelry.

• Don't wear light-sensitive glasses.

Remember that an interview is not just a one-way conversation; it is an opportunity to communicate your brand verbally and non-verbally.

Remember, your visual presentation reflects your personal brand and expertise. Ensure that your attire choice fits well, is clean and wrinkle-free, and reflects your personal style while maintaining a polished appearance.

On-Air, On-Camera and On-Stage:
This applies across platforms.
However, the stage offers more flexibility and the ability to 'go big' with your look, as there is more distance between you and the audience.

82

Which of the media training techniques has stood out to you so far? Why?

_____

_____

_____

_____

_____

_____

What do you want your appearance to say about you when you interview?

_____

_____

_____

What style and wardrobe choices can you make to communicate the above?

_____

_____

_____

_____

Master Your Body Language

How to Communicate Interest
Be mindful and ensure that your facial expressions match your words. Smile if it is appropriate. Always keep a mildly pleasant expression that says, 'I'm listening.'

An expression that looks neutral off camera can come across as unhappy or angry on-camera. A pleasant face may feel unnatural or overly 'smiley' at first. With a bit of practice in the mirror and with your cell phone camera at home, you will find the best-balanced expression for you.

What To Avoid At All Costs

- Do not nod your head to indicate that you understand or are ready to answer the question. Inadvertently, this may convey agreement with the reporter's premise, even when you do not mean to do so. Remain neutral in your facial expression and head positions. Become more animated only when you begin to speak from your key messages and zone of expertise.

- Do not speak too freely and assume the microphone, camera, or any other type of recording device is off immediately before or after an interview. Anything you say is still "fair game." It is safest to consider your entire interaction "on the record."

- Do not ask for "off the record" discussions or assume your conversations with a journalist will remain private. While journalists build a career on maintaining trusted sources, their primary allegiance is to the story. Never share anything with a journalist that you would not mind seeing in a story, unintentionally or otherwise.

- Finally, if a production team member asks you to test the sound level of your mic by speaking for a bit, say something safe. For example, talk about the weather or recite a poem. A good strategic play is to recite your mission statement and your contact information. The most popular option is to simply count from one to ten as many times as they need to be able to balance the microphones.

- Avoid the urge to be funny or say anything off-color or controversial.

On-Air, On-Camera and On-Stage:
Mastering these techniques will make you a stronger brand across platforms.

CHAPTER 9 - SHORTCUTS? ALL ABOUT PRESS RELEASES

This bonus chapter is a must.

The steps to earned media and elevated visibility do take time and strategy. You may be wondering if there is a guaranteed route to placing your brand in the media.

Some publicists have started to teach entrepreneurs, specifically, that the quickest and guaranteed way to media coverage is by using press releases.

Their reason for encouraging press releases is to get the coveted "as seen in" designation to then use across personal promotional platforms to boost credibility.

While it is exciting to say that you have been 'seen in' media including CBS, Yahoo or the like, there are issues with this method, and mindset of gaining media logos to look good.

Issue 1:

When the "as seen in," designation is listed on any of your materials, the researching party will Google this claim and search for your media hits. They will find a series of press releases written from your own point of view, posted in the general carousel of press releases of whatever online platform picked up that release.

For journalists and high performing entities that are looking for your type of service or expertise, they will see right through this as a marketing ploy. Lasting credibility is created from alignment with media through thought leadership, borrowed credibility, and increased visibility.

It is not enough to say you showed up. The key is in HOW you show up.

Issue 2:

Most press releases are written from a marketing perspective, lack storytelling, and include direct sales pitches. These documents are immediately deleted by journalists looking for experts to feature. In earlier chapters we explored that sales language is not permitted in the news space. However, these poorly structured documents can still be picked up through press releases distribution portals, or wire services.

Widely distributing content that does not position you as knowledgeable, thorough, and professional does little to boost your brand credibility.

Issue 3:
The cost. Press release distributions are done via a news wire. These services range in cost, from approximately $200 to more than $2,000, per release sent. The range is determined by the wire service and takes into consideration the reach of the distribution, and what assets you include with the release.

For example, a press release that includes a photo, video, and hyperlink, then distributed nationally will cost exponentially more than a release with no visual component, no hyperlink, and distributed locally.

Issue 4:
Outside of being able to say you are 'seen in' media outlets, there are rarely plans to leverage the press release outside of this.

As a trained journalist and executive communicator, I caution my media masters away from this method, especially if being used for the "as seen in," vanity designation reason.

However, I do think that a strategy I call "announcement blitz" can lead to the esteem and visibility a brand is seeking and avoiding the novice approach and issues above.

An "announcement blitz" is leveraging a series of strategically timed press releases to gain traction online, push your ranking up higher in online search engines, and begin to push down old or negative news. I use the "announcement blitz" when there is negative press that is just on the verge of picking up steam. I also use this tactic when a brand has been drowned out by competitors in the search results.

In support of a regular cadence of different announcements, clients are to reflect the same messaging and cadence on their platforms. Near the middle, then again near the end of the blitz, a funnel and call to action are released across platforms to capture the new eyes– or warm leads.

In short, the idea is to interrupt the search engine rankings for a moment and leverage the momentum to grow.

There are more details, nuances, and strategy to an "announcement blitz," that I personally fold in, but what has been included above is a process that has never been taught, and certainly not in any of the books or trainings I have experienced throughout the years. This is a personal ingredient in my secret sauce, part of what has catapulted my career and my clients' brands.

Additional uses for press releases include:
- To inform a media pitch to a journalist (add as an attachment in your pitch email)
- To get your event posted on media community calendars
- To distribute to organizations or supporters as an update.

Should you try the general press releases uses, an "announcement blitz," or choose to chip away time, money, and effort for an "as seen in" designation, be intentional about the content of your release.

Often press releases are written in a way that inspires journalists to immediately delete them. The headlines are not up to media standards, and they are sometimes a long, sales-y sounding tool that no one wants to read.

To ensure your press release is up to media standards:

- Keep the headline short and informative.
- Add a sub headline that is also short but adds more details if needed.
- Keep the document to one page.
- Include an overview of your brand or organization at the very bottom of the page. This is called a boilerplate. Be intentional in the messaging.
- Avoid writing the press release in first person.
- Include a quote from a spokesperson, not a testimonial from a customer.

(Tip: a customer testimonial can be positioned as a quote if the release is written strategically.)

Determine the reason for your press release, write it to media standards, and have a larger plan around the distribution of the release. Do not forget to determine a budget for the distribution and if that cost measures up to the results you are seeking.

Professionals across sectors of the communications industry seem to have a love/hate relationship with press releases. I believe that releases have a place in strategic media relations as a tool, not a solution. Remember, the role of media is to inform. Your role as a business leader is to support that goal while cultivating your audience. Press release distribution can become costly. Earned media is free.

CHAPTER 10 - IN CONCLUSION

Less of a book to be read than stored away on a bookshelf, this compilation of decades of communications strategy, trials, errors, research, and experiences aims to be your go-to guide.

By following the key strategies explored throughout this book, you will enhance your ability to capture the attention of the media and secure valuable coverage for your brand or organization.

Remember, the power of storytelling, honing your core message, tailoring your pitch to outlets, leveraging visuals, engaging emotionally, being nimble, and measuring impact is at the center of successful media engagement.

Brand leaders, speakers, and creators lean into the reflection questions and get ready to elevate to your next level of greatness.

Leaders who believe your comms teams could use support– gift those hardworking professionals this roadmap.

Publicists and communications professionals who are ready to diversify your offerings and enhance your skillset, refer to this guide as often as you would like throughout your practice.

Your story has the potential to inspire, educate, and motivate others. With dedication, strategic thinking, and this guide, you now have the power to *Master The Media*.

The Quest Media Training Team is here if you are ready to **go further and elevate faster.**

QuestMediaTraining.com/contact

For achievers who prefer the exercises compiled together with extra space for planning and notes, explore the *Master The Media* **Workbook**, found at:

QuestMediaTraining.com/resources

ABOUT THE AUTHOR: ZAKIYA LARRY

Zakiya Larry, past Global Chief Communications Officer within a publicly traded company in the advertising, tech, and creative industry, is a featured thought leader on major media platforms including: The New York Times, O, The Oprah Magazine, FOX News Radio Network, Black Enterprise, The Washington Post, ESSENCE, Ebony, and others.

A trained journalist turned entrepreneur, Zakiya is Founder and Chief Strategist of Quest Media Training, a strategic communications firm that elevates brands and awareness through strategy, media coaching, speaking and PR training, crisis mitigation and strategic public relations. Zakiya and her team also lead trainings and campaigns to create relevant messaging and committed action in response to crises and social unrest.

She has managed publicity for many blockbuster hits and New York Times bestsellers. Zakiya has also coordinated production for Oprah Winfrey, Dr. Oz and other notables. Her work has garnered no less than a dozen national and international awards, and tens of billions of earned media impressions.

Her strategy execution experience spans global brands and industries including: McDonald's, the U.S. Black Chambers, Inc., 72andSunny, Sony Pictures, and many others.

As a speaker, Zakiya has moved audiences from, in The East Room at The White House to the parliament of Johannesburg, South Africa. She has also been a featured speaker at major international events like SXSW (South By Southwest) and MegaFest.

When not helping brands *Master The Media*, Zakiya likes to spend time traveling and watching movies with her husband, Dr. Brandon L. Wolfe, an amazing soul who happens to be a Chief Diversity Officer.

Connect with Zakiya on all social media platforms @ZakiyaLarry.

www.ingramcontent.com/pod-product-compliance
Lightning Source LLC
Chambersburg PA
CBHW040929210326
41597CB00030B/5229